STEM
IS
EVERYWHERE

JOHN LESLEY

WEATHER
OR CLIMATE?

REDBACK
publishing

T0118884

Redback Publishing
PO Box 357 Frenchs Forest NSW 2086
Australia

www.redbackpublishing.com
orders@redbackpublishing.com

© Redback Publishing 2022

ISBN 978-1-922322-90-6

All rights reserved. No part of this publication may be reproduced in any
form or by any means (including photocopying or storing it in any medium
by electronic means and whether or not transiently or incidentally to
some other use of this publication) without the written permission of
the copyright owner. Applications for the copyright owner's written
permission should be addressed to the publisher.

Author: John Lesley
Editor: Marlene Vaughan
Designer: Redback Publishing

Original illustrations © Redback Publishing 2022
Originated by Redback Publishing

Printed and bound in Malaysia

Acknowledgments
Abbreviations: l—left, r—right, b—bottom, t—top, c—centre, m—middle
We would like to thank the following for permission to reproduce
photographs: (Images © shutterstock) p13b by narongpon chaibot via
Shutterstock, p23ml by Pande Putu Hadi Wiguna via Shutterstock p27b by
Amit kg via Shutterstock.

Every effort has been made to contact copyright holders of any material
reproduced in this book. Any omissions will be rectified in subsequent
printings if notice is given to the publisher.

NATIONAL
LIBRARY
OF AUSTRALIA

A catalogue record for this
book is available from the
National Library of Australia

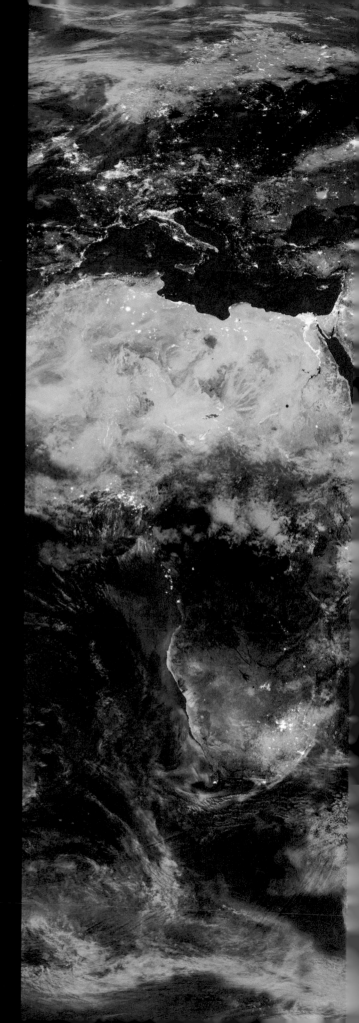

CONTENTS

WEATHER OR CLIMATE?

Weather and climate refer to the rain, sunshine, wind and temperature, but they do it in different ways. They both describe the condition of the atmosphere - the fragile, thin layer of gases that surrounds Earth.

WEATHER

Weather is what is happening right now, in the near future or recent past. When we complain about getting wet in the rain, or the temperature being too cold to go swimming, we are talking about the weather.

CLIMATE

Climate is a long-term concept. It describes the general way that the atmosphere is behaving over many months, years or even millennia.

FACTORS THAT AFFECT BOTH CLIMATE AND WEATHER INCLUDE

TEMPERATURE
The temperature of the air at ground level is different from the temperature at higher altitudes.

CLOUDS
Cloud cover that is thick will lower the temperature in the daytime but can increase it at night.

AIR PRESSURE
Areas of different pressure result in mass movements of air, creating winds.

WIND SPEED
Wind speed is low in gentle breezes but high in cyclones.

RAINFALL
Rainfall is part of the Earth's water cycle.

HUMIDITY
A high level of water vapour in the air can make us feel very uncomfortable.

CLIMATE AND LIFE

All around the world there are regions with different climates, where animals and plants have evolved and adapted so that they can survive. They make these places their homes because they are able to find food and shelter there.

Living things from one climatic region may not be able to survive if they move somewhere else. For example, a polar bear would die in a desert, but a camel can live and thrive there.

CLIMATE AND BIOMES

Add together the climate, landscape, plants and animals in a region and you get a biome. A biome is a place that can support an ecosystem.

POLAR REGIONS

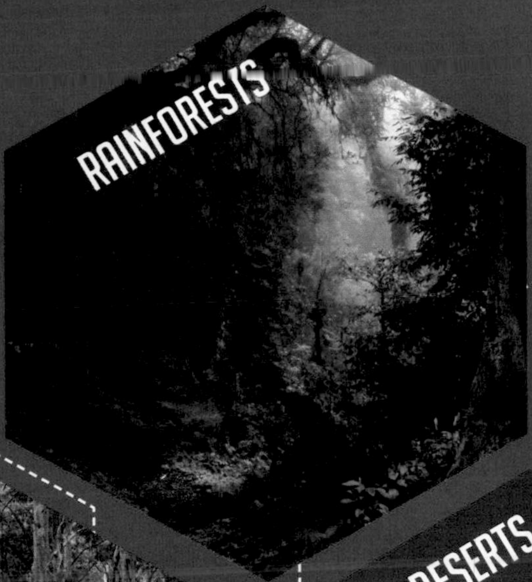

RAINFORESTS

FORESTS

DESERTS

EXAMPLES OF BIOMES

OCEANS

LAKES

ECOSYSTEM

MOUNTAINS

An ecosystem is the interaction of living thigs in a biome.

PEOPLE AND CLIMATE

The development of human communities around the world has depended on the local climate.

BUILDINGS

Whether it's a cosy igloo made from blocks of ice, or a cool, open-walled house in Southeast Asia, they all make use of local resources to provide shelter from the weather. People use whatever is available to build their homes, and the climate influences the style of building that provides the best sort of shelter.

CLOTHES

The inventions of weaving, sewing and knitting have all emerged from the need to live safely and comfortably in a particular type of climate. Ranging from garments made from fine cotton in India, to those manufactured from thick furs and leather in cold areas, the development of clothing has allowed people to live in nearly all of Earth's climates.

AGRICULTURE

Farmers in different climates around the world grow crops and keep animals that are suited to the local conditions.

CATTLE

Humans have been herding cattle for thousands of years. This long period has allowed the development of cattle breeds that differ in their ability to thrive in a variety of climates.

Brahmin cattle are well suited to hot, tropical areas, such as northern Australia. In the cold climate of Tibet, farmers keep yaks instead.

WHAT ARE THE CLIMATE TYPES?

EARTH HAS MANY DIFFERENT CLIMATE TYPES

⊙ MEDITERRANEAN CLIMATES

WHERE: Around the Mediterranean Sea and in parts of Australia and the USA
TEMPERATURES: Hot, dry summers and wet, cool winters
RAINFALL: Rain falls throughout the year, with more in the winter

⊙ POLAR CLIMATES

WHERE: North and South Poles
TEMPERATURES: Very cold with long, dark winters and cold summers
RAINFALL: Very low

⊙ HOT DESERT CLIMATES

WHERE: Near the Equator
TEMPERATURES: Very hot in the daytime and may be cold at night
RAINFALL: Very low

⊙ TROPICAL CLIMATES

WHERE: Near the Equator
TEMPERATURES: Very hot
RAINFALL: Heavy rainfall

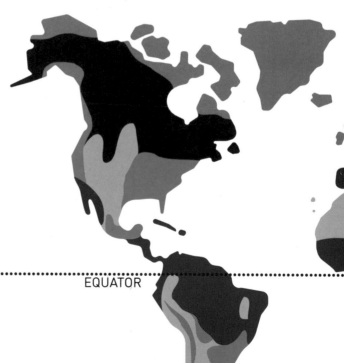

EQUATOR

⊙ TEMPERATE CLIMATES

WHERE: Areas between the tropical and polar regions
TEMPERATURES: Warm summers and cool winters
RAINFALL: Moderate rainfall, spread throughout the year

MICROCLIMATES

Microclimates occur in small or even tiny areas and differ from the climate of their surroundings.

The microclimate of a rocky place near a spring in a desert will be cooler and more humid than the desert around it. The plants and animals living in microclimates become dependent on the special conditions there.

FISH TANKS

A fish tank that you might have at home will have its own microclimate. If the water becomes too hot or too cold, the fish will get sick. The same sort of thing can happen in natural microclimates.

CLIMATE CHANGE

Climate change is a major topic of discussion and research.

One unusually hot day in winter does not mean that the climate has changed. It is only a variation in the daily weather.

If winter days are consistently hotter over a whole season, and if this continues year after year, then we can say that the climate has changed.

WESTERLY WINDS

WEAK TRADE WINDS

WARM WATER

COLD WATER

EL NIÑO YEAR

EL NIÑO AND LA NIÑA

One of the factors that alters rainfall levels and results in the possibility of drought is a regular change in the Pacific Ocean currents. This change causes weather patterns called El Niño when droughts on land are likely, and La Niña when there is plenty of rain.

STRONG TRADE WINDS

WARM WATER

COLD WATER

LA NIÑA YEAR

GLOBAL WARMING

Meteorologists can measure if temperatures around the world are changing. Working out the reason for these temperature changes is a very complex task.

There are a number of theories about why climatic regions all around Earth seem to be experiencing increases in long-term temperature readings.

CARBON DIOXIDE IN THE AIR

Extra carbon dioxide in the air can come from a number of sources. People contribute a large part of it by burning coal, petrol, wood and oil. We do this to create electricity, use our computers, drive cars, fly in airplanes, travel on ships and cook our meals. Volcanoes also spew huge amounts of gases out into the atmosphere when they erupt.

Carbon dioxide forms a blanket over the Earth, keeping heat in and stopping it escaping into space.

In the past, the blanketing effect of carbon dioxide has helped life develop on Earth by keeping the temperatures warm enough for us to live comfortably. This is called the greenhouse effect.

If there is too much carbon dioxide, the increases in normal temperatures can place living things under stress and affect their ability to survive and reproduce.

BENEATH THE EARTH'S SURFACE

Under the surface of the Earth, at its centre, is a hot ball of iron. Temperatures at the centre of the Earth can be as high as they are on the surface of the Sun. Scientists believe that very little of this heat ever reaches the surface.

INNER CORE
1600 KM

OUTER CORE
2750 KM

MANTLE
2800 KM

CRUST
50-70 KM

THE SUN

The heat that comes to us from our Sun is not constant. It varies according to solar activities that are far beyond our control.

SOLAR STORM

SUN'S SOLAR WINDS

SUN SPOT

EARTH'S MAGNETIC FIELD

CLIMATE CHANGE AND ICE AGES

The Earth's climate has been changing since the planet formed over 4.5 billion years ago. About 10,000 years ago, the last Ice Age ended, causing sea levels to rise all over the planet. People did not contribute to this climate change event, so what caused it?

Scientists think that a change in the tilt of the Earth, combined with different amounts of heat energy coming from the Sun, resulted in the beginning and end of the last Ice Age.

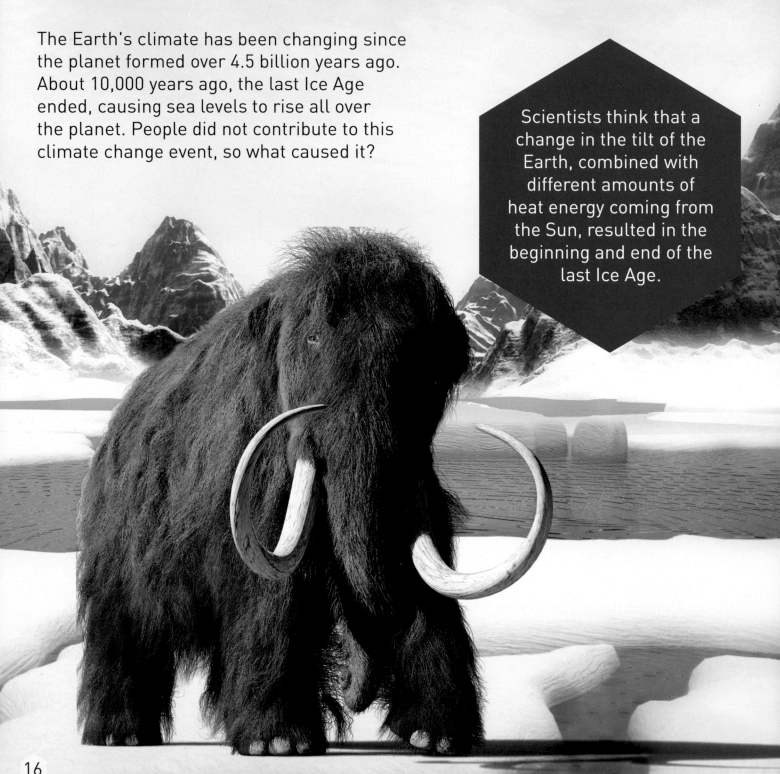

WHAT WAS EARTH LIKE IN THE LAST ICE AGE?

Ice sheets covered all of Canada, as well as the northern parts of Europe and China. Many places that are now covered by oceans were dry land. As the sea levels fell during the last Ice Age, the island of Tasmania became attached to Australia by dry land.

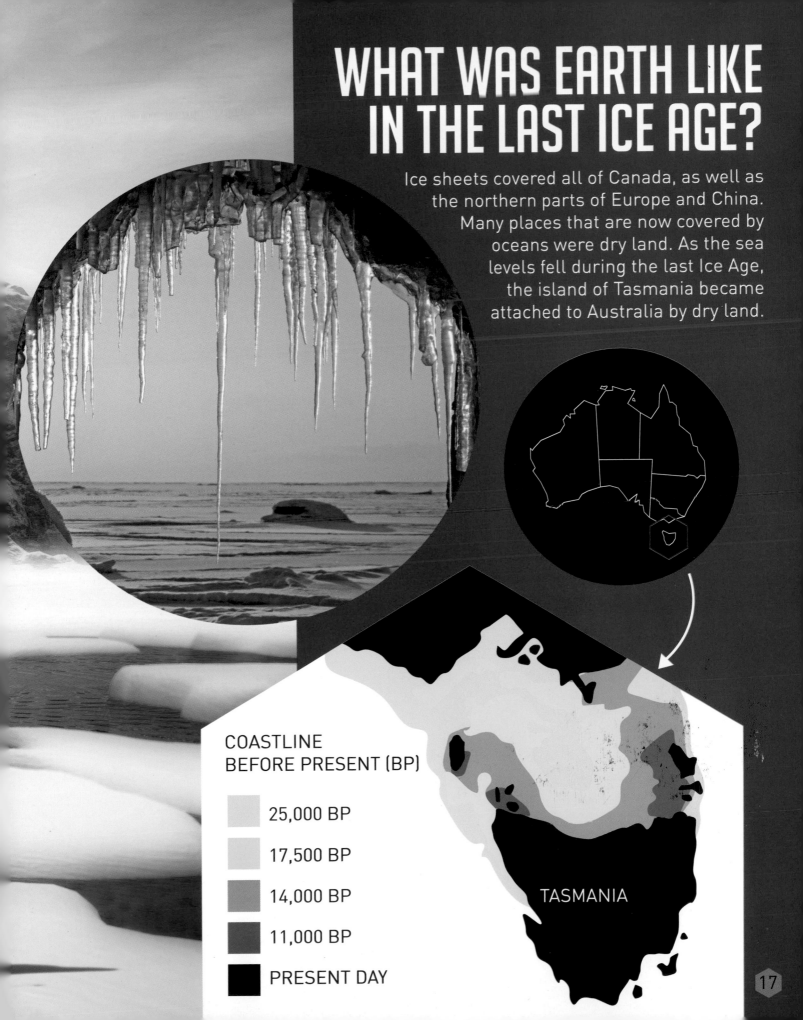

COASTLINE BEFORE PRESENT (BP)

- 25,000 BP
- 17,500 BP
- 14,000 BP
- 11,000 BP
- PRESENT DAY

TASMANIA

SEASONS

Earth is tilted slightly as it spins around. This is what causes the seasons. The tilt presents the lower part of the globe to the heat of the Sun, while the upper part is further away, making summer and winter.

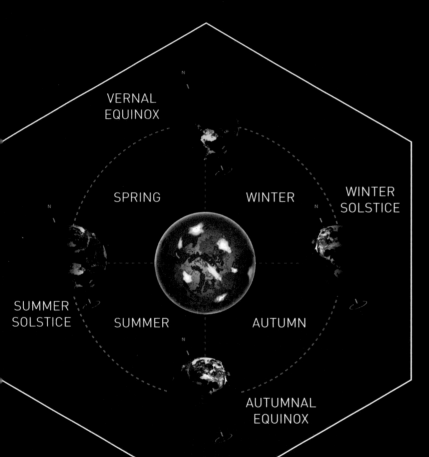

VERNAL EQUINOX

SPRING

WINTER

WINTER SOLSTICE

SUMMER SOLSTICE

SUMMER

AUTUMN

AUTUMNAL EQUINOX

As the Earth moves around the Sun, the tilt causes the northern and southern hemispheres to always experience different seasons.

In temperate climate zones there are four seasons

SPRING

SUMMER

AUTUMN

WINTER

In tropical climate zones there are two seasons

WET

DRY

BUTTERFLY EFFECT

The butterfly effect is based on a theory which suggests that even tiny events in one part of the world can eventually lead to massive events elsewhere. If a butterfly flaps its wings in one country, will this cause a hurricane to occur much later somewhere else?

MEASURING THE WEATHER AND CLIMATE

Meteorologists study the way the weather changes each day, and the way this results in changes to climate over long periods.

WEATHER STATION

Different types of measuring devices can be located in the one place in a weather station.

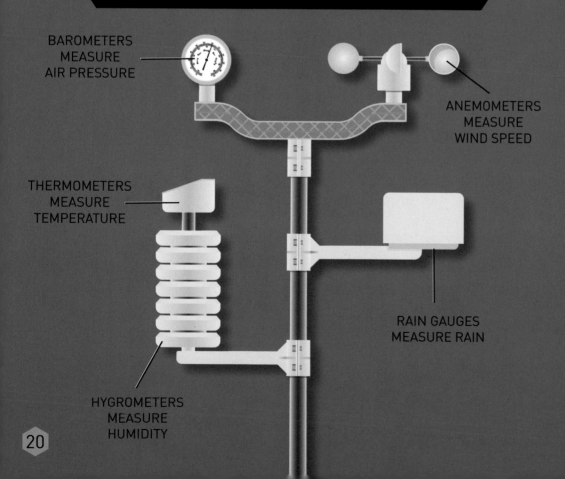

BAROMETERS MEASURE AIR PRESSURE

ANEMOMETERS MEASURE WIND SPEED

THERMOMETERS MEASURE TEMPERATURE

RAIN GAUGES MEASURE RAIN

HYGROMETERS MEASURE HUMIDITY

WEATHER OVER THE OCEANS

Some weather stations are located on fixed weather buoys out in the open ocean. There are also ships that record official weather data.

Weather stations on the oceans read the same things that land-based ones do, but they also record the temperature of the water surface and the height of waves.

PREDICTING THE FUTURE

Meteorologists can predict the future, but they use science not magic to do this.

To predict tomorrow's weather, they look at the way air masses are moving. From studying these, they can predict how the temperature will change and if it will rain.

SUNDAY	☀	32°C
MONDAY	☀	29°C
TUESDAY	🌧	25°C

WEDNESDAY SCATTERED THUNDERSTORMS
Day, Month, Year
LOCATION
23°C

Feels like: 23°C   Wind: 23 KM/H
Humidity: 63%   Sunrise: 5:52 AM
Pressure: 1012.1 MB   Sunset: 8:12 PM

THURSDAY	☁	26°C
FRIDAY	🌦	27°C
SATURDAY	⛅	28°C

Meteorologists use technology to work out what the weather will be like in the future. By combining results obtained from many sources, meteorologists can work out what the weather is likely to be in the future.

Some of the technology they use includes:

Computer programs that use all this information to create weather predictions

Radar

Weather balloons that rise into the air and collect data from high above the ground or oceans

Network of weather stations that measure temperature, rainfall, air pressure, humidity and wind speed

Satellites

WHERE DOES THE WIND COME FROM?

Wind is a movement of air. This movement can happen when areas of low and high air pressure come together. High pressure air moves towards an area of lower pressure, and the place where they meet is called a **weather front**.

As wind speed increases, we use different names to describe the movement of the air

BREEZE   **GUST**   **GALE**   **HURRICANE**

WIND HAS SPEED AND DIRECTION

An easterly wind means that the wind is coming from the east, not blowing towards it.

The wind over the oceans or high in the air is measured in knots instead of kilometres per hour.

1 KNOT =
1.9 KILOMETRES PER HOUR

WHAT CAN YOU SEE IN THE CLOUDS?

People enjoy looking at clouds and imagining what creatures the shapes look like. Is that a dragon or a rabbit in the sky?

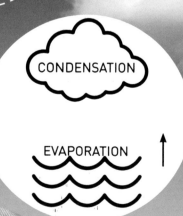

CONDENSATION

EVAPORATION

Clouds are made of water. As warm air near the surface of the Earth rises, the water vapour travels up with it. Eventually, the water vapour comes to a level in the atmosphere that is cold enough to cause the water vapour to turn into liquid drops or ice crystals that we see as clouds.

TYPES OF CLOUDS

Most of us describe clouds as white or grey, fluffy or heavy, but meteorologists use more scientific names to describe them.

CIRRUS CLOUDS

These form high up in the atmosphere. They look thin or may cover the whole sky.

CUMULUS CLOUDS

These form at the middle level of the atmosphere. They are the white, fluffy clouds that look like pictures in the sky.

STRATUS CLOUDS

These form at the low to middle level of the atmosphere. They are flat and can be dark grey, meaning that rain is coming.

WHAT ABOUT FOG?

Fog is a cloud that forms at ground level. In cities and near factories, fog can be a yellow colour and very thick due to pollution in the air.

LANDSCAPES AND CLIMATE

The shape of the landscape on the surface of the Earth can affect the weather and the long-term climate of a region.

OCEANS

Oceans play an important role in controlling the Earth's climates. When water absorbs heat from the Sun's rays, the release of this stored energy can result in changes to the weather. The heat is also distributed around the world in ocean currents.

VOLCANOES

Volcanoes that release a lot of dust into the air can cause a lowering of temperature across vast areas of the Earth's surface. This is a result of sunlight not being able to reach through the thick dust.

DESERTS

Dry deserts do not have much water to release into the air through evaporation. This is why there are not many clouds over hot deserts, unless a massive movement of water-laden air blows across the desert from somewhere else.

MOUNTAINS

High mountain ranges can block the movement of winds. As water vapour in the air meets the cold mountain tops, this can cause rain to fall as the vapour changes into water droplets.

In Australia, the mountains of the Great Dividing Range lie along the east coast are the source of many river systems. The water in the rivers comes from the rain that falls on the mountains.

DO OTHER PLANETS HAVE CLIMATES AND WEATHER?

Climate and weather both describe events that are happening in a planet's atmosphere. Planets that are surrounded by a layer of gases have weather events that are sometimes very much like those we experience on Earth.

Astronomers have seen storms on other planets in our Solar System. The Great Red Spot on Jupiter is a massive storm that has been raging on that giant planet for a very long time.

GIANT DUST STORM ON JUPITER

DUST STORMS ON MARS

The Mars Rovers have all had to deal with dust storms caused by wind on the planet. The red dust coats their solar panels, causing the Mars Rovers to shut down because they no longer receive enough solar energy to run their equipment or transmit information back to us on Earth.

RAIN ON VENUS

Venus does have rain, but not as water. The rain on Venus is made of sulphuric acid. On Earth, we avoid being anywhere near sulphuric acid, because it is so dangerous.

WORDS ABOUT WEATHER AND CLIMATE

adaptation changes in biology to make a living thing better suited to its environment

agriculture farming

air pressure force from the weight of air

altitude height above the ground

biome living things and the place where they exist

butterfly effect theory that movement in one part of the atmosphere can eventually result in a larger effect somewhere else

carbon dioxide gas in the atmosphere

ecosystem interactions of living things

El Niño, La Niña changing pattern of climate in the Pacific Ocean region

evaporation when liquid water changes into a gas

fog cloud at ground level

greenhouse effect heating of the atmosphere due to the blanketing effect of gases in the air

humidity amount of water vapour in the air

igloo rounded house made of ice

meteorologist scientist who studies weather and climate

microclimate climate in a small, restricted area

temperate having a mild climate

tropical having a hot, wet climate

weather buoy floating weather station

weather front area where masses of cold and warm air meet

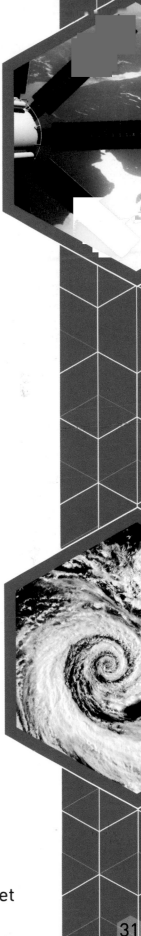

INDEX